DATE DUE

DE 21 '04			
DE 05			
MY 4 '06			
OC 12 '06			
OC 22 '07			
OC 28 '08			
JAN 29			

Demco

THE LIBRARY OF

WOLVES AND WILD DOGS™

J. D. Murdoch and M. S. Becker

The Rosen Publishing Group's
PowerKids Press™
New York

For Soir, Ditshipi, Islay, Mistral, and Cypress

Published in 2002 by The Rosen Publishing Group, Inc.
29 East 21st Street, New York, NY 10010

First Edition

Book Design: Michael de Guzman
Project Editor: Emily Raabe

Photo Credits: pp. 4, 7, 12, 14, 16, 17, 19, 22 © Hamman/Heldring/Animals Animals; p. 6 © Wolfgang Kaehler/CORBIS; p. 8 © Anthony Bannister; Gallo Images/CORBIS; p. 11 © Bruce Davidson/Animals Animals; p. 15 © Mickey Gibson/Animals Animals; p. 20 © Joe McDonald/Animals Animals.

Murdoch, J. D.
The African wild dog / by J.D. Murdoch and M.S. Becker.
p. cm. — (The library of wolves and wild dogs)
ISBN 0-8239-5769-1 (lib. bdg.)
1. African wild dog—Juvenile literature. [1. African wild dog. 2. Wild dogs. 3. Endangered species.] I. Becker, M. S. II. Title. III. Series.
QL737.C22 M755 2002
599.77—dc21

00-013011

Manufactured in the United States of America

Contents

Wild Dog Families

The African wild dog is a very social animal that lives only in Africa. The African wild dog is its own **species**, but it is related to wolves and foxes. African wild dogs live in family groups called **packs** that usually have from 8 to 15 adult dogs. Packs are like families, with a mother, father, and children. The mother and the father **mate** and have puppies every year. Other pack members usually include brothers and sisters of the parents. Each year pack members help to raise a **litter** of pups that one day will hunt with the pack.

African wild dogs look very different from wolves or foxes. They have very big, rounded ears and colorful coats. African wild dogs also have long, strong legs for chasing the animals that they like to eat.

This young African wild dog is begging for food from an adult pack member. If the adult dog has food in its stomach, it will throw some up for the pup to eat. For a hungry wild dog pup, that's a tasty snack!

Wild Dogs and Their Relatives

The African wild dog is a member of the dog family, which also is known as the Canidae family. The wild dog is related to other **canids** of the world. Canids include wolves, jackals, foxes, the coyote, the dhole, the raccoon dog of Asia, and the bush dog of South America. The canids are a very successful group of animals. They live on almost every **continent**. Ten kinds of canids live in Africa. These include the

Jackals are smaller than African wild dogs. They stand only 15–20 inches (38–51 cm) high, and weigh 15–30 pounds (7–14 kg).

African wild dog, three types of jackal, five types of fox, and the Ethiopian wolf. Many people think that the African wild dog is a **feral** pet dog. This is not true, however. Pet or domestic dogs are actually more closely related to the gray wolf than to the wild dog. The gray wolf is separated from the African wild dog by millions of years of **evolution**.

The African wild dog is the largest wild canid in Africa. It weighs about 60 pounds (27 kg), and is about 28 inches (71 cm) tall.

Life on the Edge

Sadly, the African wild dog is a highly **endangered** animal. In fact, many scientists consider the wild dog to be one of Africa's most endangered **carnivores**. Wild dogs once lived throughout most of Africa. Today African wild dogs live in only 15 of the 39 countries where they once lived. In these 15 countries, the total number of wild dogs is only from 3,000 to 5,500. This is about the same number as the number of gumballs in a large gumball machine! The main problems for African wild dogs are the destruction of their **habitat**, disease, and **persecution** by people. Many people, for example, kill the wild dogs because they are afraid the dogs will kill their sheep and cows. Some of the largest surviving groups of wild dogs are in Tanzania, Botswana, South Africa, Zambia, and Zimbabwe.

The Okavango Delta in Botswana is home to the Moremi Game Reserve. This is where one of the last African wild dog populations in the world lives.

Born to Run

African wild dogs hunt mostly in the early morning and late evening hours, when the sunlight is low. They hunt over very long distances. They sometimes travel up to 5 miles (8 km) in a morning or evening to find food. This would be like running around a city block nearly 10 times just for breakfast or dinner! Wild dogs eat many different kinds of animals, such as **impala**, **kudu**, and **wildebeest**. These animals are all large, hoofed mammals. They all can run very fast. Wild dogs must be able to run even faster to catch them. In fact, wild dogs can run up to 40 mph (64 km/h). This makes them one of the fastest land animals, not only in Africa, but in the whole world!

The African wild dog's body is built for speed, which allows it to catch fast animals like this wildebeest.

These wild dogs will eat their food peacefully, making sure that each dog gets its share.

Table Manners of the African Wild Dog

For most African **predators**, such as lions and spotted hyenas, mealtime usually includes lots of growling, snarling, and fighting over food. For African wild dogs, however, eating is very quiet and polite. All of the pack members work together. Some dogs pull apart the meal, while other dogs keep a lookout for danger. Pups in the pack almost always eat first. They are followed by their one-year-old brothers and sisters, and then by the adult wild dogs. For the first year of their lives, pups depend on the adult pack members for their food and for protection. Even though the adult members take very good care of the pups, only about half of all the pups born in a pack survive to be one year old.

Colorful Coats

It can be very difficult to see African wild dogs in the wild, even if they are very close. The reason is that they have specially colored coats, which make them blend into their surroundings. Wild dogs have coats or fur patterns that are usually brown, black, and white. No two coat patterns are the same. In fact, every African wild dog in the world has a different coat pattern!

Every African wild dog has a different coat pattern.

Some wild dogs are darker than others. Some are more brown. Some coats have a lot of white and some have almost no white at all. These distinctive coat patterns allow wild dogs to hide from animals such as African lions that might hurt or kill them. The colorful patterns also make it hard for impala and other **prey** animals to see them. This makes it easier for African wild dogs to sneak up on their prey.

The African wild dog's coat of many colors helps it to blend in with the African landscape.

Wild Dog Dens

Wild dogs have their pups in dens. Dens are large underground rooms dug in the dirt. Each year a pack's mother dog will have pups. Most years she will give birth to about 10 pups. The pups are born in the den. They will spend the first few months of their lives there. During that time, all of the other pack members will help the mother raise the pups. After hunting, for example, the pack members will bring back food in their stomachs to the den. They **regurgitate** this food to feed the growing pups. Sometimes a few pack members skip hunting to baby-sit the pups at the den. These baby-sitters guard and protect the pups from danger.

These year-old dogs are looking for their puppy brothers and sisters in the den, perhaps to get them to come out and play!

Den Life

The first several months of a wild dog pup's life are quite nice. Pups do three things at the den. These three things are eat, sleep, and play, play, play! Because pack members bring meat to the pups and guard them, the pups have lots of free time to play. Life for them is one big recess as they chase, wrestle, and play tug-of-war. Adults may even bring the pups a piece of bone, horn, or fur as a toy for them to play with! Although this may seem like pure fun, it also prepares pups for life once they leave the den. Playing makes the pups stronger and faster so they can be better hunters and pack members. Once the pups are about three months old, they leave the den where they were born and begin hunting with the older pack members.

Lessons that these playful pups learn now will help them survive when they become adults and raise puppies themselves.

How New Packs Are Formed

Sometimes an African wild dog will stay with its family pack throughout its life. Usually, however, adult dogs will leave the pack to start a new pack of their own in another area. When wild dogs try to start a new pack, they usually leave as a group of sisters or a group of brothers. These groups sometimes travel great distances to start new packs. They will travel as much as 125 miles (201 km) away from their family pack's range. That's almost like

The center dog in this picture is wearing a radio collar. Scientists put radio collars on wild dogs to track the dogs over their huge territories.

walking from New York City to Boston! New packs are formed when one of these traveling groups meets up with another group of wild dogs that has left another pack.

Pack Power

Why do giraffes have long necks? How come cheetahs can run as fast as a car can be driven? Features like these are called **adaptations**. African wild dogs have adapted to their **environment** by living in packs. There are several ways that living in a pack makes life easier for the dogs. For example, just like many pet dogs and cats, wild dogs and lions do not get along well. Living in a pack means that there are more eyes, ears, and noses on the lookout for lions and other dangerous animals. Pack members also take care of one another. If members of the pack get sick or injured, the rest of the pack will care for them and bring them food. Unfortunately, African wild dogs cannot save themselves from people who kill them or destroy their habitats. These amazing and beautiful animals need the protection of humans to survive in Africa.

Glossary

adaptations (a-dap-TAY-shunz) Features of a living thing that help it survive and reproduce better in its natural environment or home.
canids (KAY-nids) Animals in the dog or Canidae family.
carnivores (KAR-nih-vorz) Animals that eat other animals for food.
continent (KON-tin-ent) One of the seven great masses of land on Earth.
endangered (en-DAYN-jerd) When something is in danger of no longer existing.
environment (en-VY-urn-ment) The living things and conditions that make up a place.
evolution (eh-vuh-LOO-shun) A process of change and development that living things go through.
feral (FER-al) Something that was once tame but has returned to the wild.
habitat (HA-bih-tat) The surroundings where an animal or a plant naturally lives.
impala (im-PAH-lah) A medium-size antelope from Africa.
kudu (KOO-doo) A large African antelope.
litter (LIH-tur) Baby animals born to the same mother at the same time.
mate (MAYT) When a male and a female come together to make babies.
packs (PAKS) Groups of the same kind of animal hunting or living together.
persecution (pur-sih-KYOO-shun) Treating people or animals badly because of who they are.
predators (PREH-duh-terz) Animals that kill other animals for food.
prey (PRAY) An animal that is hunted by another animal for food.
regurgitate (re-GUR-juh-tayt) To vomit, or throw up, partly eaten food.
species (SPEE-sheez) A single kind of plant or animal. People are one species.
wildebeest (WIL-deh-beest) A large African antelope with a broad muzzle, a short glossy coat of gray or brown, and curved horns. Also known as a gnu.

Index

Web Sites

To learn more about African wild dogs, check out these Web sites:

www.canids.org/

www.naturalia.org/wild_dog/